LAUNDRY 101

COMPILED
BY Richard Schelske
Gary Funk

ASPEN WEST

PUBLISHING & DISTRIBUTION
8535 South 700 West Unit C
Sandy, Utah 84070
801-565-1370
www.aspenwest.com

Illustrated by Robert Betty
Article 1 Publishing • PO Box 39
Pocatello, ID 83204

TABLE OF CONTENTS

INTRODUCTION

This book is designed for college students or any novice who's suddenly thrust in the middle of the unfamiliar—laundry. Doing laundry certainly doesn't have to be difficult. In fact there are washing instructions on most washing machines, on the detergent box and even on the clothes you wash. And you do have to know which detergent to use and how much, and what temperature the water should be—then you need to know how to sort laundry so the colors won't bleed and run on each other. The purpose of this book is to bring the general information and helpful tips together for your convenience.

We make it simple: sort, wash, dry, fold and you're out of there. Now you're clean-clothed, sharper looking, fresh smelling and have a brighter outlook on life— ready to tackle trig, chemistry, or even your favorite date!

SIX CLUES

that may lead you to believe it's time to do your laundry:

1.
   Your socks leave for class 10 minutes before you do.

2.
   There's an odor about your room that a 16 ounce can of Lysol can no longer control.

3.
   When your clothes hamper looks like JAWS attacked a designer jean shop.

4.
   When you have to call the paramedics to revive your best friend who was overcome by a closet full of stinky, mildewed clothes while looking for your tennis racquet.

5.
   When the tongues on your Nikes talk to each other during class.

6.
   When a friend suggests an exorcism may be the only way to get rid of the dirty clothes haunting your closet.

AN ODE TO WASH DAY

Wash day is at hand and you begin to sort clothes in earnest. (Translation: the only clean thing left in your closet is a sweater Aunt Marge gave you for your 15th birthday, and you're seriously considering wearing it to a party or spending your last $15 bucks on a new shirt, so...you've decided it's time to face "the clothes." Ironically you think, "They've always been friendly to mother, how could they turn on me like this, they're gathering in a heap over there, I could swear I saw something move...they're getting stronger—well, the smell anyway.")

PILE 1

Pile 1 stands by itself. Needless to say it's all the blue denims—dark colored gray and black, too. Since these duds have similar characteristics and like properties, they're allowed to be a load of their own. Four to six pairs equal a load, depending on the height and girth of the owner of the wardrobe and depending on the size of the washing machine you're using. Never "pack" a machine, it's not like packing wheel bearings, not like a backpack, not like a six-pack. Just loosely fill the machine.

For a better idea of how to fill-out your jeans load:

**4 Humongous
Tight Ends**

**6 Petite
Tight Ends**

OR

**5 of Us
Regular Guys**

**=1
Load**

Blue denims are rugged, so the wash cycle normal/regular is used. Water temp: warm wash and cold rinse should give satisfactory results. Set water level to large or high for a full load. Add the amount of soap suggested on your box of detergent.

NOTE: many of today's jeans are made from cotton. Heat shrinks cotton,so washing them in hot water or drying them for hours on end will make them shrink—you'll have to lose lbs. or bequest them to your little brother.

STOP, be sure to inspect the pockets of your jeans, mom always did and besides that last stick of gum could permanently bind your fly shut or melt in the dryer in a designer pattern—and the spare change you find will come in handy this weekend. Plus you'll need those extra quarters and dimes for the dryer if you're in a laundromat.

EXTRA HINT: Zip or button up the fly (whichever the case may be) and remove any strings that can tangle up in the machine. Even though denims are rugged, a little T.L.C. will go a long way in extending their life. Washing them inside out will help retain their color too.

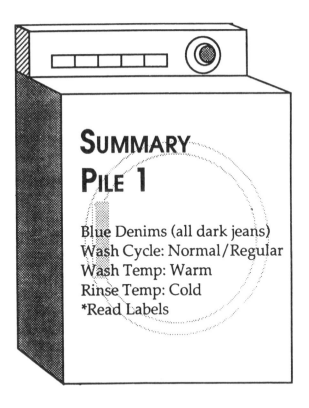

SUMMARY PILE 1

Blue Denims (all dark jeans)
Wash Cycle: Normal/Regular
Wash Temp: Warm
Rinse Temp: Cold
*Read Labels

PILE 2

Hey, can we talk? I mean, can we get a little personal for a minute?

We have some unmentionables to deal with here.

Almost everyone has underwear to launder (seriously, almost.) Gather together all your light colored underwear, whites and pastels, to form the start of Pile 2. Throw in some light colored shirts, hankies, pants, pajamas, light-weight jackets, socks, bras, slips—whatever else you may have that meets the requirement: light colored, lightly soiled (for delicate items including lingerie refer to Pile 5). Then stand back and admire your work.

The size of the pile should not exceed that of the jeans Pile 1 (no packing remember?) Loosely fill machine. If this turns out to be your largest pile and too much, you can seperate it from the all white items, to wash in another load. Water temp: warm wash and cold rinse and set the wash cycle to normal/regular for Pile 2.

OOPS, you say you found a light shirt used as landing strip for a hoagie? **No prob.** Manufacturers anticipated bumbling human error and gave birth to spray products that pre-treat the heavily soiled area before

you put it in the wash. Follow instructions on the pre-treat container, then add the garment in with Pile 2 to wash. If you don't have any pre-treat, dish washing liquid often can be used as a pre-treat on food spills, like pizza.

STOP, sorry, again inspect the pile for potential problems that may result from washing. Among these are frayed seams and loose buttons, and the ever popular DRY CLEAN ONLY. A real ego deflator would be a wayward pen going through your wash—remember tie-dieing? How 'bout just a little on everything? You'd undoubtedly create a whole new look in fashion design, but whether or not it would be accepted by the public (or your girlfriend) is another thing.

An ALL-FABRIC BLEACH **(contains no chlorine)** can be used on light colored Pile 2. It helps with tough stains and gives the clothes a brighter look (yes, that's probably how mom did it.) Be sure to follow label directions. <u>Add "all-fabric bleach" to the wash water before adding clothes</u>, so the bleach will dissolve and not come in direct contact with the clothes. Simply turn on the washer and let it fill, add bleach, detergent then add clothes.

SUMMARY
PILE 2

Light Colors: underwear, shirts, socks, pants, etc.
Wash Cycle: Normal/Regular
Wash Temp: Warm
Rinse Temp: Cold
**May use: pre-treat, all-fabric bleach, fabric softener in rinse—read directions
**READ LABELS

PILE 3

Pile number 3 is the colored clothes that you didn't put in with pile 2, other than that it's about the same as pile 2. Pile 3 includes colored shirts, pants, socks, loud underwear and pajamas— colored "sweats" are also added to this category.

At this point it's important to read labels and washing instructions on the clothes to find out if any articles need to be separated further. Any garments labeled "hand wash" should be given special attention (if you're going to dump these in anyway be careful of drying them—like "hand wash acrylic sweaters.") After you dump them in the wash, let the sweaters dry over the back of a chair instead of in the dryer—it's just as easy and will help keep "hand wash" items in new-looking condition.

Other dark or like-colored articles can be laundered together. Labels reading "wash seperately" refer to washing with like colors.

Size up the load as you did with piles 1 and 2 (no packing here, no packing anywhere, it won't get your laundry done any quicker, tightly packed laundry won't come clean, then you just have to do it over again in several loads—it only makes sense, the soap and water have to be able to get to the clothes to clean them, so no tightly packed loads, enough already.) Wash cycle on normal/regular unless the majority of items carry a "gentle wash" label, then choose gentle cycle. You may add all-fabric bleach to this load for heavy soil or to brighten colors.

SUMMARY
PILE 3

Dark Colors: shirt, pants, socks, sweats, underwear, etc.—don't include dark colored jeans, they go in pile 1
Wash Cycle: Normal/Regular
Wash Temp: Warm
Rinse Temp: Cold
**May use: pre-treat, all-fabric bleach, fabric softener in rinse-read dir.
**READ LABELS

PILE 4

Contrary to popular belief, sheets **do** need to be laundered. It's recommended that they be washed weekly…really! If you choose not to, the consequences may not be disastrous, but on the other hand, crawling into clean, fresh smelling sheets at days' end can be very rewarding.

Start Pile 4 with the sheets, add some towels, pillowcases, washcloths and you have the makings of a load. (A compatible load unless you've got dark sheets and light towels—if so, sort again.) To light colored sheets add only light colored towels, and if you've got dark colored sheets, use dark towels to fill out the batch. If you've got several small batches from each of the above, look up a friend and combine your clothes into a full efficient load. No one's going to turn down offered help with laundry and it may be a great way to get to know someone…

Towels are notorious for giving off lint, so take special care in selecting what items will be washed with them (unless you enjoy fuzzy underwear.)

Sheets and towels go in warm wash water and cold rinse water. Fabric softener is great in the rinse, follow directions. It helps the smell of moldy towels and softens the crusty ones. And it adds that fantastic scent that convinces you your time at the laundry was well spent.

SUMMARY
PILE 4

Sheets and Towels: separate colors accordingly
Wash Cycle: Normal/Regular
Wash Temp: Warm
**May use: pre-treat, all-fabric bleach, fabric softener in rinse- read directions
**READ LABELS
**Terry cloth items shed lint, take care in choosing items to wash with them.

PILE 5

After establishing the four basic wash loads and the general procedure for washing them, you'll undoubtedly find several items that haven't yet found a home. These might include blankets and washable coats, machine washable sweaters, dress pants or slacks, and nylons.

Refer to the labels on these special items and wash them accordingly. Here are some hints for these articles:

Blankets and washable coats: Wash one at a time / normal cycle / warm wash / cold rinse / fabric softener—read directions / moderate dry temp.

Washable Sweaters: FOLLOW LABEL DIREC-TIONS—if label is missing a general rule would be: gentle/delicate cycle / cold wash / cold rinse / fabric softener-read directions / cool dry temp or air dry on chair or towel.

Dress pants/slacks: FOLLOW LABEL DIRECTIONS– if label is missing a general rule would be: gentle/delicate cycle / warm wash / cold rinse / fabric softener—read directions / cool dry temp.

Lingerie/Nylons: Hand wash or machine wash with other delicate items (lingerie.) Washing nets are available to hold delicates when machine washing. Gentle/delicate cycle / warm wash / cold rinse / air dry.

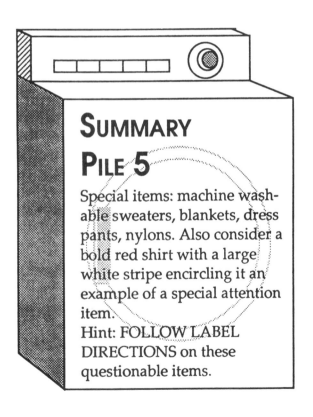

SUMMARY
PILE 5

Special items: machine washable sweaters, blankets, dress pants, nylons. Also consider a bold red shirt with a large white stripe encircling it an example of a special attention item.

Hint: FOLLOW LABEL DIRECTIONS on these questionable items.

DRYING

You have now completed the wash cycle and are ready to move on to the dryer. Here are four basic things to remember before loading the dryer: 1. Certain articles must not be dried in the dryer (check labels for instructions); 2. Inspect your clothes for loose safety pins, hairpins, etc. and tie or clip any loose strings; 3. A washer load of clothes is equal in size to a dryer load (general rule); 4. Check and clean lint filter.

Use the same methods in drying as you did in washing. For example:

PILE 1: place denims in the dryer and use the normal/regular setting. This load will take longest to dry, start checking for preferred dryness after about 45 minutes.

Pile 2: light items—separate air dry items according to label then place items in the dryer and use the permanent press or perma-press cycle if available. Be sure that you don't overdry, a good place to check is around the seams after 20-30 minutes. Hang them up from the dryer to prevent wrinkling.

Pile 3: dark items—follow the instructions for Pile 2.

Pile 4: place sheets and towels in dryer and use the normal/regular setting. REMEMBER: sheets and towels are good dryer mates because the lint from the towels will not cling to the sheets as it will to other articles of clothing.

Pile 5: the special items in this pile should be dried according to their label instructions, many of them require laying them flat and air drying.

Folding:
Hanging and folding clothes immediately after they're removed from the dryer prevents wrinkles.

Laundry can lead to a happier social life...

Doing laundry can be as exciting and rewarding as you want to make it. In addition to leaving the laundromat with nice, clean clothes, you may also leave with new friendships and new relationships. Here's a bit of advice for you guys.

If you are feeling a little unsure about doing your own laundry and happen to notice a fellow launderer of the female persuasion who catches your eye, the first thing to do is to establish a look of confusion on your face. Pick out a washing machine near her, so she can't help but notice you.

Set your wash bag down and start sorting your clothes–forget *LAUNDRY 101*— mix your whites with your colors. If she is beginning to stare, pick up your dirtiest jeans, white dress shirt, a pair of red socks and place them in the washer. Begin a detailed reading of the detergent box and shake your head and mumble a little. Your face should express confusion and helplessness—be sure she has a good view.

At this point, if she has not come to your rescue, bring out that "dry clean only" jacket you've packed just for this occasion and add it to your wash load. Surely by now human compassion has overcome her delight at your idiotic show and she'll come to your aid. Pretend not to notice her and reach for that container of liquid bleach. It should be more than any red-blooded American woman—fresh out of Home-Ec—can stand. The rest is up to you.

Now if this sounds just a tad sexist to you, maybe not your style, you can always try the reverse approach: use the laundry expertise you've gained from *LAUNDRY 101* and offer gallant assistance to your fellow launderer…walking into the sunset smelling fresher, looking brighter.

THANKS LAUNDRY 101!

Please feel free to contact Aspen West Publishing Company about our other fine products or quantity discounts.

ASPEN WEST

PUBLISHING & DISTRIBUTION
8535 South 700 West Unit C
Sandy, Utah 84070
801-565-1370
www.aspenwest.com